loving you was suicide

Logan Duane

loving you was suicide

Copyright © 2024 Logan Duane

All rights reserved. No part of this book may be reproduced
or used in any manner without the prior written permission of the copyright owner,
except for the use of brief quotations in a book review.

To request permissions, contact the author at
loganduanepoetry@gmail.com

Instagram:
@logan.duane.poetry

Other Books By Logan Duane:

the things I didn't say in therapy

words for tired hearts

loving you was suicide

*For my
fellow
survivors.*

loving you was suicide

loving you was suicide

Content Warning:

This book contains depictions of suicide, suicidal thoughts, sexual assault, sexual violence, domestic violence, body dysmorphia, child abuse, depression, Post Traumatic Stress Disorder, mental illness, toxic relationships, disordered eating, and self-harm.

Reader discretion is advised.

Your mental health matters; always take care of yourself.

loving you was suicide

loving you was suicide

Table of Contents

loving you was suicide .... pg. 8

empty bottles of SSRIs .... pg. 50

a letter to me, from me .... pg. 84

loving you was suicide

loving you was suicide

Content Warning: domestic violence, sexual violence, suicidal thoughts, toxic relationships

loving you was suicide

You were a noose

disguised
as a necklace

and I
wrapped you around my neck
despite feeling
the air
slowly escaping
my lungs.

-{loving you was suicide}

loving you was suicide

The words
"I love you"
fell from your mouth
and crumbled on the floor
like glass.

You picked up the
broken pieces
and used the sharp edges
to carve holes
in my tender heart.

-{the love that shattered me}

loving you was suicide

I have been trapped
in this cage
for so long that
it feels like

home.

-{*delusional*}

loving you was suicide

Your mask
melted away
like hot wax down your face
as you became comfortable
with treating me
like a convict
in my own home.

loving you was suicide

Remembering how
you used to be
is slow,
agonizing
torture.

All the
acts of service,
little gifts,
compliments
and laughter-filled adventures
are now tainted by
love bombing
and manipulative intentions.

You hid every red flag
behind calculated lies,
with the only goal of
molding me
into a servant
of your narcissism.

loving you was suicide

Take a bow,
fade to black.
The performance is
over now.

You don't have to act
like you love me
anymore.

loving you was suicide

Accuse

Accuse

Accuse

but never take the blame.

"You're insane"
"You're too angry"
"You're impossible to be around"

It's so easy for you
to point fingers
instead of admitting that

you
broke
me.

loving you was suicide

It was fun

until my darkness
inconvenienced you

and I didn't satisfy
your savior complex
anymore.

-{I was nothing but a game to you}

loving you was suicide

We hang on
to all the wrong things
to keep our souls
from shattering.

loving you was suicide

I finally grasped
how dire
my situation had become
when I saw
a casket
as my only feasible
escape.

loving you was suicide

I paused for a moment
at the front door
and noticed an
ever so familiar
ache
in the pit of my stomach.

I caught myself feeling
nauseous at the thought
of being forced to maintain
the happy partner
facade

and I wept.

How long
has it been
since home
felt like home?

loving you was suicide

This bed we share
feels so
lonely

these days.

loving you was suicide

Your love for me
waxed and waned
with the cycle
of the moon;

but your gravitational pull
was so enticing
that I threw away
my need for
stability.

-{part-time love}

loving you was suicide

Like lidocaine on my lips

I was numb
to the bitter taste of
poison
when we kissed.

loving you was suicide

I loved you
so fiercely
that I became
complicit
in the cycle of
narcissistic abuse
that you
put me through.

loving you was suicide

Embarrassment
flushes my cheeks
as I look back
and think about
all of the excuses
I made for
your bullshit.

loving you was suicide

You had me convinced
that I would die without you

when you were the one
draining the life
from my veins.

loving you was suicide

You were
the darkest night,
the coldest winter,
the most painful love,

and the hardest goodbye.

I just keep reminding myself
that if I can make it
through being with
you

then I can make it
through
anything.

loving you was suicide

I am worth more
than the
empty,
passionless "love"
that we share.

loving you was suicide

I placed my palm
to your chest
and the coldness of your heart
pierced through my skin
and turned my bones
to ice.

-*{I used to be so warm}*

loving you was suicide

Your broken heart
convinced you that
we were in love

when really
you just wanted to cling
to the first warm body
that gave you
attention.

-*{you never truly loved me}*

loving you was suicide

You thought that
I would die here

and for a moment,
I did, too

but I've come
too far

survived
too much

to ever give you the
satisfaction
of being the one
to nail my coffin
shut.

loving you was suicide

Who am I
if not
your prisoner
anymore?

loving you was suicide

I can't give you
what you want

because your heart aches
for someone who
is everything
that I am not.

-*{I can't be them}*

loving you was suicide

Fuck you
for making love
feel like
a weapon.

loving you was suicide

"No one will ever love you."

The words ring in my ears
as my fatigued body
melts into the floor
beneath your weight.

"I'll make sure everyone knows you're a whore,"
you say;

at least, I think that's what you said.
I can't hear you over the sound
of my heart
pounding in my throat.

"Go ahead and write another rape poem.
No one will believe you anyway."

Your voice
feels like knives
in my lungs.

-*{just another statistic}*

loving you was suicide

Why didn't you
stop
when you saw
tears
hit my pillow?

-*{my pain got you off}*

loving you was suicide

You lurk around
every corner

stalking me

hunting me

waiting for me
to give up
and succumb to your advances.

My mind goes numb.

My body aches.

My soul screams for someone to
make it stop

but at least you're satisfied,
right?

-{betraying my body}

loving you was suicide

I shouldn't have to
beg you
to love me
when my
clothes are on.

loving you was suicide

You could
strangle me
with your bare hands

and I would apologize
for not being able
to breathe.

loving you was suicide

I'm so fed up
with half-hearted promises
and cheap,
late night
apologies.

loving you was suicide

I flew
headfirst
into the sun

and then wondered
how I got
burned.

-{blissful ignorance}

loving you was suicide

Your mouth whispered
"I love you"
while your eyes screamed
"you'll never be good enough."

loving you was suicide

There you are

knocking
knocking
knocking

at each corner of my mind,
pushing every button
with the only intention
of driving me
to insanity.

loving you was suicide

too fat
too thin
too loud
too quiet
too stubborn
too boisterous
too opinionated
too stupid
too slow
too aggressive
too needy
too talkative
too much

too much

TOO MUCH

-*{I can never get it right for you}*

loving you was suicide

I wanted
a calm, ocean breeze
kind of love

but you crashed into me
like rogue waves
until the day I finally
drowned.

-*{I never stood a chance}*

loving you was suicide

You have
no place here
anymore.

-*{preserving my peace}*

loving you was suicide

We were
two lovers
in universes parallel
to one another -

never crossing,
never touching,
never sharing time or space.

-{our love was not meant for this life}

loving you was suicide

You are
incapable
of love.

I see that now.

Just don't expect me
to continue
hanging around,
waiting for you
to give me the heart
that doesn't exist
within your chest.

-*{I'm worth so much more than that}*

loving you was suicide

If you ever
cared for me at all,

let me walk away
with what is left
of my
tired, aching
soul.

-*{if you ever loved me}*

loving you was suicide

The moment that I stopped
begging for your
approval

was the moment
you started
panicking -

scrambling to piece together
lies and scare tactics
to prevent me from
seeing the truth.

I saw fear
in your eyes
as I realized
I don't need you.

-*{never have, never will}*

loving you was suicide

empty bottles of SSRIs

Content Warning: suicidal thoughts, self-harm, sexual violence, sexual assault, body dysmorphia, mental illness, child abuse, PTSD, disordered eating

loving you was suicide

I will never be able
to rid myself
of the venom that
plagues my mind.

It will consume me
from the inside out
until there's nothing left of me
but
broken memories
and empty bottles of SSRIs.

loving you was suicide

Pain
courses through my veins
as naturally as
the blood
that keeps me alive.

loving you was suicide

If spring never comes
and my body gets lost
in the icy, unforgiving grip
of winter,

plant flowers
at my bedside
so my soul
never knows
winter's pain.

-*{if the seasons never change}*

loving you was suicide

The turmoil in
my head
is so loud
that I swear
I can feel each part of my brain
melting into a river
of my sorrows.

-*{make it stop}*

loving you was suicide

If I can't bear
to wake in the morning
and I never get to see
another sunrise,

bury my bones
where her rays
touch the earth

so my soul
can rest
in her warmth.

-*{if this is my last sunrise}*

loving you was suicide

My sanity is being
held hostage
in the
caves
of my brain.

loving you was suicide

I find myself struggling to
break the cycle
of self-destructive lows
and euphoric highs.

-{the comfort in chaos}

loving you was suicide

I fight with
the same
four pounds
that fluctuate
on and off
my body

as if the problem
is my weight
and not my
desperate need for
control.

loving you was suicide

For once
I want to step on the treadmill
for pleasure,
and not with the intention of

punishing myself

for eating
three full meals.

loving you was suicide

A child
should have
no concept of

diets
laxatives
beauty standards or
restrictive eating.

No child
should look in the mirror
and hate their
reflection.

loving you was suicide

You could show up
at my bedroom door
tonight,

rock me to sleep,
sing me a lullaby,
read me a bedtime story

and I would easily
forget
about all of the years
I shed tears
waiting for you
to comfort me
like that.

loving you was suicide

I don't have many
happy childhood memories.

I don't have many
childhood memories
at all.

-*{amnesia}*

loving you was suicide

I was a blank canvas
and you were
the artist.

With sharp strokes
of acrylics along my skin,

you painted me
to look like
an ugly,
unforgivable monster
that you could
throw away
and disown
with horrifying ease.

loving you was suicide

She's been a servant
to your sadistic,
cynical ways
for so long
that you and her
don't look so
different
anymore.

-*{I needed her to save me}*

loving you was suicide

I will forever
grieve
the parent that I needed you to be -

the parent that
he murdered
when you took
his last name.

loving you was suicide

I'm on my
hands and knees
desperately pleading
for you to look me in the eyes
and see the beast
that you've created.

I'm screaming so loudly
that blood runs from my ears
in hopes that
you'll finally hear
something I say.

I'm breaking my own bones
just so you'll come
glue me back
together

but you don't.
You never do.

You're too busy
nursing your ego
to ever notice that
your daughter
is dying for you
to care.

-*{I've always been invisible to you}*

loving you was suicide

It didn't make me stronger.

It gave me PTSD,
a drug addiction,
and years of hurting myself
just to feel something.

I didn't need strength.

I needed to feel safe
in my own home.

loving you was suicide

I vividly remember
how your feet sounded
as they crept down the halls in the night,
and how I would
hide under the covers
until I heard the
click
of your bedroom door
as it closed behind you.

I can still smell
the chewing tobacco
that rested in your
bottom lip.

I still feel your
lifeless, cold eyes
glare at me from across the room
like I was nothing but
a useless,
good-for-nothing
waste of space.

-*{Oh, how I wish I could forget}*

loving you was suicide

"You're so mature for your age"
is something they tell
little kids
who are raised
in the dark shadows
of a narcissist.

-*{forced to grow up}*

loving you was suicide

Sometimes I lie awake in bed
in between cold, sweaty nightmares
and wonder if you wish
that you had
two children
instead of
three.

-*{least favorite daughter}*

loving you was suicide

I was just a
little girl

but your cold,
sweaty hands
claimed my body
like I was
fully grown.

-*{the death of her innocence}*

loving you was suicide

My body tells stories
that my mouth
wouldn't dare to
speak of.

-{he lingers on my skin}

loving you was suicide

I am so tired
of dancing around the word
rape
as if I am dirty for
saying it out loud,
and he's not to blame
for forcing that word
into my
vocabulary.

loving you was suicide

How is it fair
that you get to continue
living a cozy,
joyful life

and I am forced
to relive
everything you did to me
over
and over
and over
and over
with no promise
that it will ever
stop?

-*{I crave justice}*

loving you was suicide

Do you fall asleep at night
reminiscing about
all of the dreams
you so selfishly
stole from me
with your
venomous touch?

Do you look at yourself
in the mirror
and feel proud
of the deranged,
malevolent reflection
that stares blankly
back at you?

Do you find peace in knowing
that I
still flinch
at the sound
of your name?

-*{how do you live with yourself?}*

loving you was suicide

I want you to know

that I still
fucking hate you

for preying on me
while I was so
vulnerable.

loving you was suicide

No matter how many times
I touch a blade
to my skin,
I can't forget
what it felt like
for my body to belong
to someone other than
myself.

-*{get him off of me}*

loving you was suicide

I despise
who I had to
become
to survive
in your
presence.

loving you was suicide

I feel the warm,
familiar blanket
of apathy
wash over my body
as your words
echo in my ears.

I find myself
slipping away from reality
with each vile insult
that falls from
your lips.

I've grown too tired
to beg you to stop,

so I allow my brain
to safely
tuck me away
into nothingness
instead.

-*{you can't hurt me here}*

loving you was suicide

I will write my name
in blood
across your chest
so that every time you look in a mirror
you're forced to remember
how many times
I bled
for you.

loving you was suicide

PTSD
is like having
your trauma
branded onto your skin
with scorching hot irons
each and every time
you're reminded of

what

happened

to

you.

loving you was suicide

I am forced
to live with the fact
that I am
permanently
changed
because of your actions.

-*{not fair}*

loving you was suicide

I guess I'll keep taking

medication

after medication

after medication

if it releases me
from the torture
of remembering
you.

loving you was suicide

a letter to me, from me

Content Warning: mental illness, sexual assault, child abuse

loving you was suicide

You are loved.

You are whole.

You are worthy of
safety,
forgiveness
and joy.

You deserve to recover,

and I will say it
over and over
until you believe it.

-{a letter to me, from me}

loving you was suicide

To the person who
stitched my mouth shut
with hatred and lies
so no one could hear my story -

this one's for
you.

loving you was suicide

A shower so hot
that it burns your skin
will never wash away
the memory
of him.

-*{you are not dirty}*

loving you was suicide

All I can do
is keep begging the universe
to give you
what you
deserve.

-*{I hope it fucking hurts}*

loving you was suicide

"No"
is not supposed to
feel like
a dirty word.

loving you was suicide

The road is long
and agonizing,

but I have never been
more determined
to make you
nothing but a
hollow memory.

-*{the process of healing}*

loving you was suicide

You would keep my obituary
like a trophy.

You'd hang it on the wall
above the shelf of
all your prized possessions.

It's too bad
I'll never give you
the opportunity.

-*{I survive just to spite you}*

loving you was suicide

The absence of
you
has allowed for me to
bloom
in the most
magical way.

-*{if you could see me now}*

loving you was suicide

My happiness
is not yours
to steal for me
anymore.

-*{I'm taking it back}*

loving you was suicide

If I could
turn back time,

I never would have allowed myself
to lose the most
beautiful parts of my soul
just to keep you around.

loving you was suicide

I grieve for the parts of me
that will never be the same,

the parts of me
that will never come back,

the parts of me
that I have long forgotten.

I grieve for the little girl
who will never know peace,

the little girl who
just wanted to feel loved,

the little girl who
I destroyed just to suit your needs.

loving you was suicide

Don't ever let anyone
convince you that
you are not
whole.

-*{you are complete}*

loving you was suicide

Allow yourself to
feel your feelings.

Embrace them,
love them,
tend to them,
cry with them,

and then give yourself permission
to let them go.

-*{stop running}*

loving you was suicide

How do you grieve
a version of
yourself?

-*{I want to lay her to rest}*

loving you was suicide

Lying to myself
was so easy
that I couldn't see
how quickly
my soul was
dying.

-*{it's time for authenticity}*

loving you was suicide

For as long as I live,
I will never
allow myself
to be anything
except for genuine

ever again.

-*{promises to myself}*

loving you was suicide

For the first time in my life,

I am
so close
to being the version of myself
that I have always
dreamed of being.

loving you was suicide

Breaking your own heart
will never
make
them
love
you.

-*{let them go}*

loving you was suicide

The feeling of
comfort
tugged at my raw,
throbbing heart
as I went to
walk out
for the final time.

But darling,
comfort
is not
love.

loving you was suicide

When this is
over,

I hope that they
can finally see
the pernicious effect
you had on every
piece of my
battered soul.

loving you was suicide

At first,
I thought you
hung the moon,
painted the stars
and danced with the tides.

You were the perfect storm
in a too-convincing
disguise.

-*{I'm not so easily fooled anymore}*

loving you was suicide

I will write about you
until my fingers bleed
if it saves the next girl
from falling victim to your
selfish games.

loving you was suicide

I can only hope
that one day
you'll allow yourself
to rest
in the palm of my hands
so your world doesn't
feel so heavy
anymore.

loving you was suicide

I grew from
the ashes of
the home he
burned.

loving you was suicide

I refuse
to raise my child
in a home where
mom
eats a different meal
than everyone else
because she's terrified
of the numbers
attached to food.

-*{it ends now}*

loving you was suicide

Once I started
truly loving myself,

I realized that
I am not nearly as
hard to love
as I have been made
to believe.

-*{I am worthy}*

loving you was suicide

Thank you
for teaching me
how to survive
when every part of my soul
felt like
dying.

-*{silver linings}*

loving you was suicide

I have wasted
so much time
merely existing

not living

and I refuse to continue
catering
to things that
suppress my ability
to finally

experience life.

loving you was suicide

For the first time
I find comfort in
the feeling of
my beating
heart.

-*{I fell in love with life}*

loving you was suicide

I will not
devalue myself
just so that I am
more digestible
to those who
don't deserve
my presence.

loving you was suicide

As I watch
winter's last snowflake
melt into the
budding spring ground,

I am reminded that
winter never lasts forever

and happiness will bloom
again.

-*{the seasons will change, and so will I}*

loving you was suicide

As a mother,

I can't even begin
to imagine a world
in which I would

turn
my
back

on my son

just to
save face.

-{how dare you}

loving you was suicide

You used to tell a younger version of me
that having short hair
made me ugly -

that it made my face
look too round
and accentuated
all of my flaws.

Today, I took
the scissors
above my shoulders
and shed the weight of
your words
with each strand of hair
that hit the floor.

loving you was suicide

Learn how to
keep yourself safe,
even in moments when
safety
feels like
prison.

-*{your life matters}*

loving you was suicide

There are so many versions of me.

All at once,

I am a child who
is in desperate need of
comfort
and protection,

a teenager who
rebels
and lashes out,

and an adult who
lives as an
empty shell
of everything she
could have been.

I will shower each
fraction of me
with safety,
compassion,
and love -

that is how healing
begins.

loving you was suicide

In my dreams,

you are a bird
in flight -

free from the anchor
that he bound
to your feet.

In my dreams,

I am always
the one
that you choose to
fly home to.

-*{dear mom}*

loving you was suicide

I never lost myself.
I've been here the whole time,
overshadowed by
the person that I had to become
to endure the hellscape
you trapped me in.

-*{finding my voice again}*

loving you was suicide

Healing could only take place
when I admitted that
I was not ready to let go,

because letting go meant
that you were
really
gone.

-{living with grief}

loving you was suicide

Thank you for showing me
that prioritizing myself
is beautiful,
courageous,
and necessary for
the wellbeing
of my child.

loving you was suicide

I've been hardened by people
who never deserved
my soft, gentle
nature.

loving you was suicide

Most of healing
is being afraid -

afraid to be vulnerable,
make delicate decisions,
and remove yourself from toxic situations.

I promise you
that on the other side
of that fear,
there is a beautiful life
waiting for you
to be brave enough to
reach for it.

loving you was suicide

The sweetest,
most satisfactory
revenge
comes from
healing the wounds
they burdened you with

and coming out
stronger
on the other side.

-{become the hero you need}

loving you was suicide

Let the pain come.

Let yourself feel it
so intensely that
for a moment,
you think it might
kill you.

Then, get up

and prove to yourself
that you have the power
to withstand
anything.

loving you was suicide

Breathing becomes
easier
when you let go
of what
makes your lungs
feel like
cement.

loving you was suicide

I am delicately learning
how to
reparent
the child that
still exists inside of me.

-{she deserves peace}

loving you was suicide

The fragmented parts
of me
are melting together
and becoming someone
so brave
and so resilient
that you wouldn't
recognize her
anymore.

-*{becoming me}*

loving you was suicide

You can continue living
in the same lifeless box
to protect everyone around you,
or you can choose

freedom

authenticity

bravery

The choice is yours -
it's always been yours.

You can continue to settle,
or you can be happy.

-{dear people-pleaser}

loving you was suicide

There will be people
who try to convince you that
protecting your peace
and your wellbeing
is harmful
or wrong.

Those people
don't deserve to know
the healed version
of you.

loving you was suicide

The process of healing
will hurt
in unexpected
and complicated ways.

Keep going.

You deserve to meet
the person you will become
on the other side
of recovery.

loving you was suicide

I wish that I could
reach into the past,
grab

5-year-old me

10-year-old me

14-year-old me

19-year-old me

by the hands
and tell them that

we

survived.

-*{it's all going to be okay}*

Printed in Great Britain
by Amazon